Professor Plausible's Big Book of Baloney

A. B. PLAUSIBLE, Ph.D.

ISBN: 1494834820
ISBN-13: 978-1494834821

DEDICATION

This book was inspired by my students. In the past year, I have received research papers whose bibliographies included such sources as a golfing manual, a thriller set in the Vatican, and Leadership Lessons from the Dog Whisper (sic). I have tried to convince my budding scholars that popular books are not to be relied on as research sources, as they are far from infallible. There is no requirement that a book be fact-checked or peer-reviewed; with the advent of easy self-publishing, it doesn't even need to be spell-checked.

One fateful day, I exclaimed to my class that I could throw together a book of my own made-up facts, and put it up for sale on Amazon tomorrow. Would you use that as a source for your paper? I asked. The glazed looks that I got in response gave me an idea. I decided to step aside and let the rock roll back down the hill.

Behold the Big Book of Baloney: The only [citation] you'll ever need.

CONTENTS

Professor Plausible's Writing Tips	i
Notes	1
About the Author	151

PROFESSOR PLAUSIBLE'S WRITING TIPS

Always start your paper with "In today's modern world," "Since the beginning of time," or "Throughout history." This will establish that you are capable of seeing the "big picture."

Make sure to insert the dictionary definition of the topic under discussion. This is a clever device that tells the reader that you have done your research.

Preface pivotal claims with a reassuring phrase such as "everyone knows." What reader could question an idea expressed with such certainty?

Semicolons make you look smart; use them whenever possible;

If it sounds right, it probably is..

NOTES

ABOUT THE AUTHOR

Adamant Bellwether Plausible is the pen name of a real professor who teaches at a public university in one of the United States. Professor Plausible would really prefer that students—indeed, people in general—base their conclusions upon reliable sources, and not believe everything they read.

www.ingramcontent.com/pod-product-compliance
Lightning Source LLC
Chambersburg PA
CBHW080322300526
45791CB00021BA/2966
* 9 7 8 1 4 9 4 8 3 4 8 2 1 *